H.T. LAWRENCE

TRADE THE TRADER

The Ultimate Guide on How You Can Trade Like a Pro,
Discover How to Create the Perfect Mindset
For Successful Trading

Descrierea CIP a Bibliotecii Naționale a României
H.T. LAWRENCE
   TRADE THE TRADER. The Ultimate Guide on How You Can Trade Like a Pro, Discover How to Create the Perfect Mindset For Successful Trading / H.T. Lawrence. – Bucharest: Editura My Ebook, 2020
   ISBN

H.T. LAWRENCE

TRADE THE TRADER
The Ultimate Guide on How You Can Trade Like a Pro, Discover How to Create the Perfect Mindset For Successful Trading

My Ebook Publishing House
Bucharest, 2020

TABLE OF CONTENTS

Foreword 7

Chapter 1: *Introduction* 9

Chapter 2: *The Mindset And Trading* 13

Chapter 3: *How To Trade On The Forex* 17

Chapter 4: *Have Realistic Expectations* 20

Chapter 5: *Understand The Power Of Patience* 24

Chapter 6: *Be Organized In Your Approach To The Markets* 29

Chapter 7: *Why Emotional Management is Critical to Trading Success* 34

Chapter 8: *Over Complicating Forex Trading Can Easily Induce Emotional Trading* 37

Chapter 9: *How Price Action Trading will Cure Emotional Trading Problems* ………….. 41

Wrapping Up: *The Winning Traits Of A Forex Trader*.. 45

FOREWORD

The aim of this book is to give readers a brief overview on Forex markets from the means through which traders can develop the proper mindset when trading, how to trade on the Forex market, why emotional management is critical to successfully trading on the Forex market, to discussing some of the favorable qualities a good Forex trader should posses. These aspects of Forex trading will be discussed in depth in the other chapters that follow but for now, we tackle the basics pertaining to Forex trading as a money making entity.

Get all the info you need here.

Forex Fortunes Guide

Create The Mindset Your Need Trade Like A Pro

CHAPTER 1

INTRODUCTION

Synopsis

Forex, abbreviated as FX, is a word that describes the simultaneous selling or buying of currencies; it is an OTC (Over the Counter) Market transaction which operates 24 hours a day, 5days a week. Forex Markets are the largest financial markets possessing a trading volume of about $3 trillion per day. Forex trading operations take place in all the major financial trading centers all over the world; thus, these trading operations tend to overlap into the different time zones globally.

The Basics

Forex means the process of exchanging one currency for another based on the market's exchange rate with these currencies being sold and purchased in pairs. For instance, for you to purchase Japanese Yen you have to sell US dollars and as a result Forex currencies have to be quoted in pairs for example GBP/USD, EUR/USD, or EUR/JPY. Some currencies have more demand than others meaning that that those with more demand trade more frequently and are referred to as major currencies.

Some of the major currencies include the Swiss Franc, Japanese Yen, British Pound, Australian Dollar, and US Dollar, whereas the less frequently traded currencies are called minor currencies, these are the currencies used in small developing countries, others refer to them as exotic currencies. Currencies commonly used as investment vehicles are confined into four pairs of currencies denoted by USD/CHF, GBP/USD, USD/JPY, and EUR/USD.

Where Forex Trading Takes Place

In the past, Forex trading was exclusively conducted by hedge funds, central banks, multinational currency companies, and major banks however; this has changed in recent times due the latest surge in internet development and market innovations allowing even the small time trader the opportunity to participate in the Forex market. Some

Forex broker companies offer a variety of accounts to their clients enabling retail traders the chance to trade in relatively smaller lots.

Even though Forex markets have undergone some remarkable improvement, it still remains largely unregulated; and Forex trading rules have not yet been clearly defined especially when trades go beyond international borders.

Furthermore, traders with a sizeable amount of risk capital as is the case with hedge funds and banks which have the ability to influence the Forex market due to their huge financial leverage; therefore, those with little or no experience in Forex trade will be venturing into risky unchartered territories.

In as much as Forex trading carries very high risks, traders who go through the trouble of educating themselves on the whole process could quite easily make a huge fortune in just a few weeks, with those doing the contrary getting disastrous results amounting to huge losses.

CHAPTER 2

THE MINDSET AND TRADING

Synopsis

Forex trading can be highly lucrative especially if you are equipped with the necessary trading knowledge and skills. Apart from possessing trading skills, it is essential to have the right mindset for you to be successful in Forex trading.

This is the crucial aspect where most traders fail. No matter how good you are in utilizing various trading strategies but without the right mindset, you might not be able to achieve the desired results.

Some would think that trading success happens in an instant and that they can easily make money out of it overnight. Although there is some truth in this belief and it is not next to impossible, only those who continuously develop effective trading habits coupled with the right trading mindset can actually prosper. Here are the best tips that you can use to ensure success in Forex trading.

Steps

Step 1: Set Realistic Expectations

The initial step is to set realistic expectations. Of course, all people would want to earn profit. In this kind of business where currency trading is highly volatile, you win some and you lose some. Chances are, if you use the right strategies and forecast, you can definitely earn a huge sum. But on the other hand, you can also lose your money.

Basically the point here is to hope for the best outcome and anticipate the worst case scenario. There are still many factors and other market forces that can directly and indirectly affect currency trading. Make sure that you do not stake your whole life on the line just to be in the Forex trading business. It is strongly suggested that you trade using the disposable risk capital, the spare money that you can use for any trading ventures.

Step 2: Trade Wisely- Quality over Quantity

It is a common misconception of some traders that they have to trade everyday just to optimize their earnings. The truth of the matter is that, you can further elevate your earnings if only you will learn how to be more patient in trading. If you really want to achieve long term success and get to explore the markets, you need to learn how to trade using daily charts.

Along with learning how to properly use these daily charts to your advantage, you start to develop your trading mindset where you have to patiently wait for the right timing. Once you have calculated risks and you think you have the trading edge then that is the perfect time to make the decision.

Step 3: Be Organized in Your Approach

Learning the market forces that affect the movements in any trading system takes a while. Without any organized approach, you might end up losing your money. Before anything else, you need to come up with your own trading plan and trading journal.

This allows you to trade with discipline and to be more organized when it comes to your trading activities and trading options. Monitoring your daily trading journal enables you to assess your performance and monitor your earnings as well.

Last but not the least, use the price data and other relevant information before you trade. Be decisive in your trading decisions and always go for calculated risks.

CHAPTER 3

HOW TO TRADE ON THE FOREX

Synopsis

Since Forex is by far the most popular trading world of currency, it also connotes that one should be able to understand the factors involved in the trading process to truly garner profit from it. If you were one of the people who want to fit in and moreover, standout in this market, then some of the tips below would help you get a head start.

Understanding the Jargons of the Market

Jargons are basically the terms used in a certain company. To be able to understand the whole process, then one should take the time to integrate what the terms mean. The basic of these are the *'base currency'*, the term for the currency one is spending or is trying to get rid of. This works primarily by selling one currency so you can actually buy another type of it. The *'exchange rate'* is the term you look at when you want to know how much you would spend to buy base currency from your quote currency. These are just some of the terms found in Forex trading.

It is also important for you to decide on the two primary currencies that you want to buy and sell. Thus, just like any other businesses, you should be consistent in the quality of your task. Therefore, staying at one exchange rate would possibly entail bigger profits.

Opening an Account

A brokerage account is an important part of the exchanging currency business. You firstly have to consider the reliability of the broker you choose to open an account to. It is advisable to research about the broker's background and how many years have he or she been in the industry. In addition to this, you should also be able to identify the broker's transparency through asking some of the people that also has an account.

Start your Trade!

This step is the most important part of this business. Once you started your venture and has done steps 1 and 2 for preparatory, be not complacent and still take time to analyze the market before you proceed to the trade itself. The technical, fundamental and sentiment analyses should be considered. Technical means reviewing and researching on some charts regarding the trades. Fundamental is taking a bird's eye view of the economic fundamentals of different countries, and thus using this to your advantage in choosing the right currencies. Lastly, the Sentiment analysis entails the mood of the market.

Never forget that every step you take can lead to the destruction or the progress of your trading. It is good to take risks but it is better to always be cautious about it. Do not just engage in this trading venture because you thought it will be easy, every step is counted and therefore must be taken into full consideration.

For whatever it costs, also always be reminded that businesses are risks; but if you take the risks with the proper weapons of knowledge about how it will and can turn out, it usually pays off at the end.

CHAPTER 4

HAVE REALISTIC EXPECTATIONS

Synopsis

Starting out in Forex trade is never an easy thing. With the promise of high investment returns, a lot of people are easily enticed to venture in currency trade without having second thoughts. After all, who would not want to double or to triple their money? For some, this might appear as the easiest way for financial liberation. Forex trade can definitely make it possible for you to earn more.

When you come across Forex trading websites, almost all would promise you converting your money into millions in just a short span of time. Some online advertisements would even beguile you to finally quit your job and to just focus on Forex trade.

But is it really worth it?
Can you really make it big overnight?

Why Set Realistic Expectations

The answer is both a yes and a no. Forex trading is definitely worth your effort especially when you already possess the right mindset and you use effective trading strategies. But the promise of earning thousands or even millions overnight is just impossible and even dangerous.

When you finally set to venture in currency trade, setting realistic expectations is the initial step. Success in this kind of business all starts with knowing what to actually expect. Since there are different market forces that can directly and indirectly impact currency trade, you can never be 100% sure.

Always keep in mind that any investment involves certain level of risks. It is basically the same thing when it comes to Forex trade. Without a doubt, you can earn a huge sum. But on the other side, you can also incur losses. Once you come out thinking that you can have all the economic gains by just buying and selling currencies, you are doomed to fail.

Remember that just like in kind of investment venture, you need to be realistic to make your goals achievable and feasible.

Your attitude and mindset towards Forex trading certainly affect your trading decisions.

Calculating Risks in Forex

Instilling impossible expectations towards Forex profitability can negatively affect your trading choices. For one, traders who have high and impractical expectations might end up gambling their money without even thinking of the risks.

The tendency is that some would easily want to get high profits in an instant. There are even traders who would trade currencies everyday thinking that by doing so, they can earn more. With Forex trade being a highly volatile business venture, you can never afford to trade without even calculating the risks and without any Forex knowledge. Doing so will not only lead to disappointment but to high losses as well.

If you really want to make it in this kind of business, you need to have patience. You have to set realistic expectations so that you can carefully plan your trading strategies.

Study the currency market, gather the price data along with the significant indicators and create your trading plan. These are the things that you should keep in mind if you really want to be successful in Forex.

The expectation of earning huge amount in an instant might seem appealing at first. But in the long run, you need to understand the fact that success takes quite some time. With Forex, patience is definitely a virtue. You need to know when to use your bullets to your advantage. In that way, you can avoid incurring losses and you get to earn high profits.

CHAPTER 5

UNDERSTAND THE POWER OF PATIENCE

Synopsis

A lot of people make huge losses in Forex markets just because they make simple mistakes like overtrading or not being patient enough to allow their trade setups to play out and instead they enter and exit the Forex market compulsively. The problem may lie not so much with your trading strategy but with your inability to exercise patience by waiting for the best low risk opportunity with the highest probability of success. The tips discussed below will help any trader step up their trades from mediocre trading to consistent and profitable trades.

Educate Yourself on the Forex Market

It is important that new traders educate themselves on all matters pertaining to the Forex Market resisting the impulse to rush into trades before understanding the ins and outs of the trade. Learning through mistakes on the Forex market could leave you counting your losses, but lucky for you this can be avoided by taking the time to study the market. After clearly establishing your trading edge, you can now exercise patience by waiting for the right moment to execute your trade; patience is worthless unless the trader knows what they are waiting for.

Create a Trading Plan and Stick to It

The best traders in the market always plan ahead and are prepared at all times having compiled an elaborate trading plan after which they always act according to their plans.

Creating a plan does not necessarily mean that they trade all the time; novice traders usually accumulate losses because they think that they should be on the market trading all the time. Preparation is an important aspect to any successful trade but at times it's better to sit tight and wait for the trade to play out; just because the Forex market is open 24/7 does not mean that you should be trading all the time.

Wait for Your Trade Setup to Play Out

Good traders never anticipate how their trades will play out, those who do lose a lot of money in this manner. Exercise patience when your trade plays out and bear in mind that a good trader can be compared to a lion, an amazing predator due to his great stalking skills, and a patient one at that, always waiting for the perfect opportunity to go for the kill and what's more when he goes for it he rarely misses.

Jesse Livermore once said that big money is made by sitting and waiting, and never by thinking, he adds that it's important to wait for all the factors to tilt in your favor prior to making the trade.

Trust Your Instincts

Accurate gut feelings are indisputable with one of the greatest Forex traders, George Soros revealing that he depended heavily on his instincts when he traded.

Soros said that he relied on his animal instincts and that when he suffered from back pain he used the onset of the pain as a sign that something was wrong with his portfolio. This will prompt him to check whether something was amiss when he might have done the contrary, if he had ignored his instincts he might have incurred huge losses.

Know When to Call it Quits

If during a trade you realize that things are not going well for you it will save you a great deal of money to retrench rather than adding on to your losses by waiting for your fortunes to change. To stay in the trading game, you have to be strong enough to bear the profits and the losses and take George Soros as an example. It didn't matter to him whether he lost or won, if the trade didn't go well, he was still confident that he had the capacity to win other trades such that he could confidently walk out without any hard feelings.

CHAPTER 6

BE ORGANIZED IN YOUR APPROACH TO THE MARKETS

Synopsis

The phrase "playing the market" may make it seem like you would enjoy greater success by trusting your gut instincts, going with the flow, and being a slave to trends. However, the truth is actually the opposite. You have better chances of earning from Forex trading if you adapt a more disciplined and organized method when trading.

Avoid letting your emotions and all the hype get the better of you with the following tips.

Planning is still the key to success

If you remember your Management 101 lessons, then you should know that Planning is the first step to success. Forex trading is no exception. You need to come up with plans for your short-term and long-term goals. These plans also have to be detailed. If possible, include step-by-step guidelines for how you want your strategy to work out.

Focus on a few high-potential currency pairs.

Don't spread your resources thin. It's hard to put your plan and strategies to good use when you have a lot on your plate.

Rather, it's better to take your time choosing a small number of currency pairs that you can fully focus on and nurture until the very end.

The more time you spend studying how your pair works in the market, the more chances you have of predicting its *future* trends. Consequently, you'll have a *lesser* need to rely on instincts alone when making a decision. Instinct is not a bad thing at all, but instincts powered by knowledge are even more trustworthy.

Use a timetable.

A timetable can be a more powerful tool than an ordinary calendar if you know how to make good use of it. To start with, take note of all the important events that are relevant to your trading plan and strategies. These include but are not limited to the following:

- Public holidays in *both* countries where your currency pairs originate
- Global and economic summits affecting your currency pairs
- Economic releases

- Scheduled key announcements from major market players

All the events above are sure to affect your currency pair in terms of demand, supply, and liquidity – just to name a few. Every time you add an event to your timetable, remember to review your plan and strategies and adjust them accordingly if it proves necessary.

Expand your network.

When it comes to any kind of trading, it's who you know, what you know, and when you know that matter. Being able to predict market trends is a great skill, but it's not one you can always rely on. However, what you can be sure to depend on at all times is your network. It's fairly easy to determine which individuals will make good sources for insider's information. The challenges lie in making those individuals a willing part of your network.

Check technical analyses.

Technical opinions must always be taken into account even if you strongly feel the opposite of what these experts have to say. At the end of the day, you need to remind yourself that technical analyses are based on verifiable facts and figures. They *have* to mean something.

Last but not the least, remember that your ultimate goal is to minimize your loss first and increase your profit next. *Don't* gamble everything on a whim.

Be man enough to admit when you're on the losing side and just start again. At least you still have something to start with unlike other traders, who have lost everything because of their inability to keep their emotions in check.

CHAPTER 7

WHY EMOTIONAL MANAGEMENT IS CRITICAL TO TRADING SUCCESS

Synopsis

Trading in the foreign exchange market is not all about strategies. Oftentimes, it can involve a lot of emotions especially when the experience is not at all pleasant. After all, even when the system of trading is reliable, human factor still remains as the major player. The trader can be very effective in maximizing the potentials of the trading system.

It is also possible that the trader might lack certain qualities that prevent him in making the right approaches. It becomes even more disadvantageous when the trader lacks patience in dealing with losing trades. Thus, it is essential to control strong emotional urges ensure that the process of trading is managed properly.

Proper Emotion Management can Lead to Better Calls

There are instances wherein a trader dismisses the signs that his ways are inefficient, thinking that it is the system that is at fault. When this happens, the trader will continue with the trade, hoping that the system will eventually turn out for the better. On the part of the trader, this kind of reaction can be translated to as being optimistic. However, unless the trader is already an expert in the Forex market and he has the right resources that will validate his moves, this reaction is actually an act of stubbornness more than anything else.

The trader is given two paths- to recognize what is happening or to maintain blind optimism. When the trader recognizes that the pattern is not going to favor his end anytime soon, the best decision would be to cut losses short. Acknowledging the technicalities of how the market works will prevent the trader from experiencing any more marginal losses.

It is quite observed from novice traders that they are too hopeful when they enter the Forex market. Although optimism can be a good thing, failure to identify negative signs while they are happening will undeniably slow down the trader's progress in this volatile industry.

Patience Yields Better Results

On the other side of the spectrum, it is also important to keep emotions in check when good things are happening during the trade. However, a normal reaction from a trader who is new to the system and has immediately acquired profit would be to withdraw them at the first sign. After all, liquidating the profits will translate to guaranteed earnings.

A good lesson that amateur traders can get from experts in the system would be to let their profits run. It is true that seeing the first sign of profits will make a novice trader excited to cash out on his earnings, but if he really wants to succeed in the system, he should learn how to play along with it.

With familiarity, guidance and patience, the trader can still expand his profits while letting it run its course. The trader can study past trends so it will be easier for him to recognize the signs that the market is about to reverse. Once this occurs, he can liquidate his profits which he allowed to mature to its best potential.

CHAPTER 8

OVER COMPLICATING FOREX TRADING CAN EASILY INDUCE EMOTIONAL TRADING

Synopsis

These Forex trading tips are for those currently experiencing losing streaks, it is not unnatural for a trader to lose money once in awhile, but when you realize that you are making fewer profits and losing more, you may have some deep underlying issues you need to fix before you can get back on track. After reading this book, traders will learn how make the trading process as simple as possible, providing them with the insight on how to make more profits in the markets.

Mastering Your Mind

The primary reason as to why a lot of Forex traders are losing money is that they are unable to consciously master their emotions and it does not take long before they are deeply caught up in emotional trading mostly because the latter is easier and is more exciting than controlled trading. In essence, Forex markets offer traders a pair of options, the first one being to recklessly gamble your hard earned money away in the adrenaline packed rollercoaster trades or the ability to master your emotions through discipline, slowly making consistent money over a period of time.

A disciplined trader has the proper trading attitude which allows them to grow their investment without necessarily having to resort to risky games such as emotional trading.

Implementing the Tools for Proper Money Management

It is important that you first understand how to manage your money on the Forex trade and then later on you can proceed to implement the latter in you trading mannerisms. A lot of traders become very emotional when trading because they either trade too frequently or risk too much of their money.

Risking huge sums of money in any given trade subconsciously makes the trader to inherently place more meaning or value on every trade; since they have plenty to lose which naturally causes them to worry more thereby becoming more emotional about the Forex trade.

This kind of emotional trading works to fuel itself because emotional trading results in more emotional trading. If it so happens that a trader loses a significant sum of money, they put themselves in a vulnerable position of carrying on with the cycle because they tend to feel a great deal of anger and frustration over the lost money. This only fuels their desire to risk more money so as to try to make up for the money they had lost earlier.

Traders often mismanage their Forex trading accounts by trading a little too frequently and as a result they tend to lose way too much in a relatively short period of time. Over trading could be an emotional outlet for the trader and for them it is a form of gambling, to prevent yourself from overtrading it is important that you have a comprehensive trade risk management plan which should specifics on the means through which you can preempt overtrading.

Mastering Your Trading Strategies

It is important that any successful trader masters their Forex trading strategies, considering the fact that a lot of traders are unsure of what it is they are searching for in the market, so as to avoid inducing emotional trading.

CHAPTER 9

HOW PRICE ACTION TRADING WILL CURE EMOTIONAL TRADING PROBLEMS

Synopsis

Kingdoms have fallen and battles have been lost the moment men let their emotions get the better of them. Since the world's greatest warriors and kings have fallen prey to their own emotions, how can mere traders avoid the same death trap?

The answer is simple: it's all about having the right mindset. Consequently, price action trading is a good foundation to use for developing the right mindset. This system consists of several fundamental principles.

Focus On Managing Your Emotions Instead Of Ignoring Them

Emotions are *not* your enemy. This is extremely important to understand. Ignoring them will not help you at all. If anything, they will simply make you more prone to bad trading decisions. What's more critical is being the master of your emotions with the right mindset rather than the other way around.

Avoid Overanalyzing Forex Trading

Some traders are so opposed to the involvement of emotions in their trading strategies that they go to the extremes and over analyze their next steps. Again, doing this will only backfire on you. When you overanalyze and even overcomplicate your trading strategies and market trends, you will simply end up confusing yourself.

Remember that every complicated equation can be broken down to various simpler equations. In fact, it's one of the golden rules when writing algebraic equations: the simpler, the better! It's the same with Forex trading. If a system proves too complicated for you, then forget about it! If it works for another trader, good for them! But don't let that sway you into knocking your head against the wall. There are many other systems you can try – and some of them will surely prove much more suitable to your personality and preferences.

Stay Objective

If you succeed in emotional management, then you will be able to use your emotions to help you stay *objective*. With emotional management, you'll know which emotions to believe in more. If you are presented with a very high-risk investment that you do not understand but your friend recommends, what should you do? Greed will tempt you to bet on it, but your instinct for danger will warn you against doing something foolhardy.

With successful emotional management, you will be able to take the more objective middle ground instead and that's to carefully research your options before making any decision.

Constant Training And Practice Leads To Permanent Habits And Mindsets

Consistency and constancy are essential in making price action trading a permanent part of your mindset. It's not enough to know how price action trading works. It's not even enough to be aware that emotions can have a positive and negative impact on your life. You should also make a conscious effort to apply your knowledge to your trading decisions. It's all right to forget these principles once in a while, but don't let that hinder you from trying again.

Having the right mindset will not make your strategies fail-proof, but it can significantly reduce your risks of incurring heavy trading losses. With the right mindset, you become more aware of the pros and cons of your decision and that's more than what you can say about other traders.

Wrapping Up

THE WINNING TRAITS OF A FOREX TRADER

In the world of Forex trading, the most successful traits a trader may have has nothing to do about who gets to play the good or bad guy. Rather, it's all about the traits that increase your tendencies to make wise – or unwise – moves.

Cut Your Losses Early

Traders hear this very sage advice all this time, but most ignore it – to their everlasting regret. *Hope* is a powerful motivator. And it's always good to be optimistic. However, you have to be careful about choosing what to be hopeful for. Cutting your losses early does not mean you're quitting. It simply means it's time to move on and try another currency pair. It really is that simple.

Don't Fix What's Not Broken

It is a cliché, but that doesn't stop it from being true. In fact, ignoring clichéd advice is quintessential example of how people insist on leaving the path to success in order to take a wrong turn. Why put a stop to an account that's doing well? Although there's a chance for trading pairs that are doing so good to plummet and suffer a huge drop in their rates, these things rarely happen without any noticeable signs. In most cases, you will have enough clues to warn you and fall back to Trait #1: cutting your losses early.

Know The Right Time To Trade

Some people just like being the exceptions to the rule for the sake of it. However, that kind of attitude is dangerous for a Forex trader to adopt. More often than not, it will lead to heavy trading losses, enough to break the bank for good.

Timing is everything in Forex trading. You may like to think it as a subjective factor, but studies show that timing is actually objective. Numerous experts have proven with their case studies that the best time to trade in the Forex market is between 1900h – 1100h in UK time, which in Eastern Time will be around 1400h to 0600h.

Know The Best Times To Use Trading Breakouts Versus Range Trading

Rather than letting mere instinct to be your guide, there's a surer way of determining which of these two essential trading strategies is best to use.

- Range trading is best to use during *active* hours as your strategies are given sufficient time to work.
- Trading breakouts are best to use during *volatile* hours as they can take advantage of the extreme changes that currency pairs will undergo.

Make Use Of An Effective Leverage

How much leverage you allow yourself to use will always have a considerable impact on your trading strategies and its eventual outcomes. There are many different formulas you can use to compute how much leverage you can afford to use, but at the end of the day the factors listed below will prove most important.

- Keep it conservative.
- Always apply a stop-loss point to your strategy.
- Risk tolerance levels do not have to be proportionate with leverage.

There are always exceptions to the rule, and those are simply an inevitable part of the game. Even if things do not go your way, the above traits will serve to minimize your losses and increase your winnings.

www.ingramcontent.com/pod-product-compliance
Ingram Content Group UK Ltd.
Pitfield, Milton Keynes, MK11 3LW, UK
UKHW022213230426